AutoFocus
GRILLES & TAILS

Auto Focus

GRILLES & TAILS

Don Spiro

FRIEDMAN/FAIRFAX
PUBLISHERS

A FRIEDMAN/FAIRFAX BOOK

©2000 by Michael Friedman Publishing Group, Inc.

Please visit our website: www.metrobooks.com

Library of Congress Cataloging-in-Publication Data available upon request.

ISBN 1-58663-027-X

Editors: Ann Kirby-Payne and Alexandra Bonfante-Warren
Art Director: Kevin Ullrich
Designer: Dan Lish
Photography Editor: Kathleen Wolfe
Production Director: Maria Gonzalez

Color separations by CoulourScan Overseas Co. Pte. Ltd.
Printed in China by Lefung-Asco Printers Ltd.

1 3 5 7 9 10 8 6 4 2

Distributed by Sterling Publishing Company, Inc.
387 Park Avenue South
New York, NY 10016
Distributed in Canada by Sterling Publishing
Canadian Manda Group
One Atlantic Avenue, Suite 105
Toronto, Ontario, Canada M6K 3E7
Distributed in Australia by
Capricorn Link (Australia) Pty. Ltd.
P.O. Box 6651
Baulkham Hills, Business Centre, NSW 2153, Australia

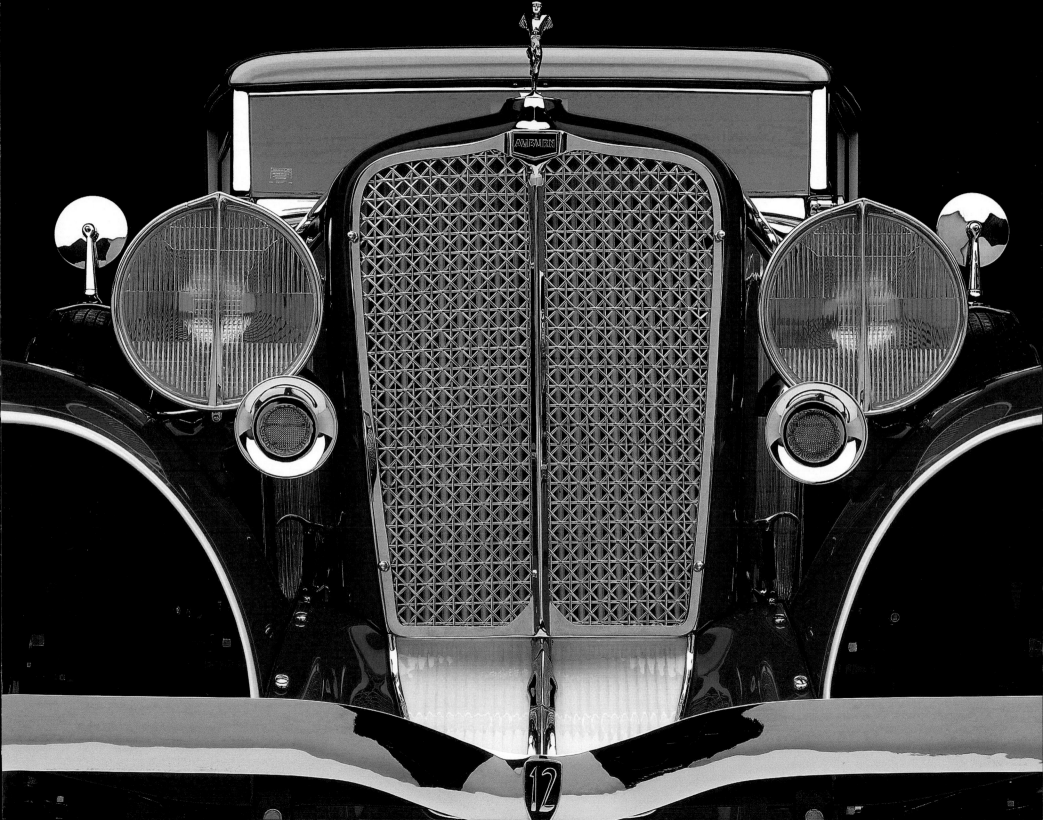

Contents

Introduction
The Beginning and the End

Once upon a time, a vehicle was readily identified by the face it put forward, the smiling grille or pointed nose that shouted its make and model to everyone who passed it. Similarly, distinctive rear ends—be they the ostentatious, heavily chromed fins of the 1959 Eldorado or the sharklike back ends of the first Sting Rays—left a lasting impression on the minds of those drivers left in their proverbial dust.

In today's competitive automotive market, where most small independent manufacturers have been swallowed up by the six or so major companies in the world, the industry has become sadly homogenized. In order to remain competitive, designers' artistic hands are often tied by budget and manufacturing requirements, and, as a result, most cars are virtually indistinguishable from others in their class. While upscale and expensive specialty cars have retained recognizable features, choices for the everyday driver are often drawn from a seemingly endless stream of bland, lookalike models. Lined up side by side, it's hard to see any difference between a Honda and a Toyota, a Ford and a Chevy.

There was a time, though, when the design of grille and tail was highly regarded as the introduction to and end statement of any new car. These features at once defined and reflected precisely for what and whom a particular car was made. In much the same

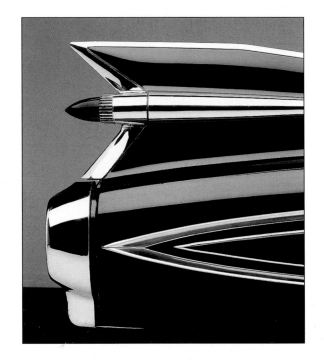

Above: The 1957 Chevy sported exhaust outlets under the fin inspired by those on jets.

Opposite: This prewar Alfa Romeo features tasteful Deco design, combined with a touch of dash proper to their racing successes of the period.

way that basic genetic material can be recombined into an infinite variety of faces, the myriad design details for the front and rear ends of cars have been reinterpreted, reinvented, reapplied, and recombined over the years into a plethora of unique cars. They have ranged in looks from beautiful, stately, and elegant to mediocre, obnoxious, and, yes, even ugly, but they were almost always something to see.

In the 1910s and '20s, the grille of a car was first and foremost a functional element—it housed the radiator, a bit of equipment vital to the cooling of the engine. In most cases, those early grilles were unremarkable, as form took a backseat to function. But there were a few notable exceptions, among them the beautiful examples produced by Rolls-Royce. The meticulously handcrafted, mirror-finished grilles—surmounted with the signature "Spirit of Ecstasy" mascot perched atop the radiator cap—seemed to be the premier design element of the Rolls-Royces of the 1910s. All Rolls models that followed for decades to come seemed to be designed around this grille.

In the 1930s, as the Art Deco movement began to take cultural hold, streamlined, Machine Age–inspired motifs began to dominate design themes on everything from household toasters to steam locomotives to architectural wonders such as New York's Chrysler Building. The Deco movement, which incorporated graphic elegance tempered with an industrial sense of pure function, was an attempt to bring art and fine design to manufactured goods, and, by doing so, to capture the spirit of speed and optimism that was the essence of the era. As such, Art Deco and automobile design grew hand-in-hand, and artistic flights of fancy came to life on the drawing boards and assembly lines of a number of car manufacturers.

Nowhere was this marriage of art and design more evident than at the vehicle's front end. From the forward-peaked prow of the late-'30s Graham Sharknose to the streamlined, sloping grille of the 1934 Chrysler Airflow and the elegantly laid-back grille of the 1934 French Citroën Traction Avant, some of the most beautiful grilles of the era, American and European both, mirrored the global obsession with Art Deco.

Strangely, the Deco aesthetic so evident in the designs of the 1930s and early '40s did not really influence the rear ends of cars until some time later. Simplicity of form reigned longer out back on most cars, and simple taillights mounted on or into the rear fenders were sufficient for most designs of the prewar era. Gradually, however, the Deco movement brought the tails in line with the sleek designs on the front end. High-end automobiles of that era—including Cords, Duesenbergs, Auburns, and Packards—were rolling works of art from one end to the other. Cars like the '39 Lincoln Zephyr made a stunning statement from the edge of the front bumper, over the curvaceous lines of the body on back, and down to the streamlined tail treatment. In beholding a Zephyr Coupe, to this day, one cannot help but be taken aback by the design's timeless quality.

After World War II, some of the more famous designers of the Deco era, notably Raymond Loewy, found themselves at the helms of automotive design

studios. Loewy would ultimately perfect some of Studebaker's finest postwar cars. Indeed, it was during the decades immediately following the war that grilles and tails reached their zenith. This was especially true of the heavily chromed, aircraft-inspired cars that rolled out of the design studios in Detroit.

Harley Earl, the brilliant chief designer at General Motors during the late 1940s and '50s, is credited with first applying the aircraft "fin" to an automobile: a 1947 Cadillac show car. During the war, Earl had been taken by the beauty of the P-38 Lightning "twin boom" fighter plane. In 1947 he incorporated small fins onto the rear of a Cadillac; although subtle when compared to what was to follow, those little bumps caused quite a stir when they first appeared, and for the next decade or more fins would become an integral part of the Cadillac's design. Those small fins would grow in form and stature each year, reaching

their oversized and razor-edged apogee on the gaudy 1959 Eldorado.

Virgil Exner was a noted designer who learned his craft under Earl's tutelage. Exner went on to Chrysler in the 1950s; there, he reshaped grilles and tails, adding fins and changing the profile of many of the cars in the company's stable. His efforts raised Plymouth's sales to the number-three spot, and his Chrysler 300 sedan brought slab-sided and high fins to the forefront of design.

Never in the history of auto design were fins and grilles designed with the kind of wild, childlike abandon that defined 1950s American auto design. By today's standards, those flamboyant and whimsical elements seem garish and even gaudy, but in the aftermath of depression and war such overly chromed and finned leviathans were an authentic reflection of the prosperity of the times, and the possibilities of the future.

By the early 1960s, fins and grilles had peaked, and designs were becoming more conservative. The towering fins that had been so admired on the 1957 Chevy seemed to have collapsed under their own weight by 1960; they now lay horizontally across the deck lid in peaceful repose. Aerodynamic considerations in the late '60s and early '70s brought about the "kamm back," or chopped-off tail treatment—where once fins rose majestically at the back of a car, there were now flat expanses of sheet metal stretching across the back with taillights at each end.

Grilles, too, became less ostentatious and more integrated, with sleek, aerodynamic styling. Shapes that defined automakers—such as BMW's twin kidney-shaped grilles, Mercedes's classic square radiator housing, and Pontiac's large, square center grille flanked by sleek twin grilles—all shrank proportionately. Fuel economy dictated the clean aerodynamics that cut down resistance so that the car could knife through the air. Even staunch traditionalist Rolls-Royce, whose tall, square, regal grille had been its longtime calling card, shrank and rounded off its trademark in the name of aerodynamics.

The 1980s saw the beginning of the end for the traditional grille on many manufacturers' models. Ford's bold and daring design statement, the Taurus of 1986, dispensed entirely with a grille in favor of a small, futuristic, elliptical opening, featuring its Blue Oval suspended within. This would soon become the signature front-end treatment at Ford, across most model lines and into the new millennium.

Such changes were not limited to Detroit's Big Three. When, in the early 1990s, Bugatti resumed production with its superfast and aerodynamic E-100B, the classic horse-collar Bugatti grille became merely

a very small horse collar–shaped opening, set down low in the center of the car's front end. It was a mere hint of the once magnificently identifiable Bugatti grille that had adorned every model from the Type 57 to the rare and wonderful Type 41 Royale.

Aerodynamic designs and improved airflow through sleek ducts rendered the flashy grilles of decades past obsolete. In the decades to come, automobiles might have minimal openings up front, and a shape that will offer the very least resistance to wind in the name of fuel economy. Yet some new cars—notably Ford's 2000 Thunderbird—hint at days of old with retrostyled grilles and subtle tails that serve form more than function. Could the times be changing once again?

The 1937 Alfa Romeo 8C 2900B combined streamlined Art Deco styling with performance that was legendary on tracks such as the Targa Florio and Le Mans.

Smiles and Sneers
Classic Grilles and Noses

The late 1940s and early '50s saw a certain degree of temperance in grille treatments, no doubt an evolutionary carryover from the 1930s. Nevertheless, in an industry that had been perfecting planned obsolescence, the grille was a feature that could be easily changed, creating a new look for each model year. Among the most radical were the bullet-nosed Studebaker Champions and Commanders of the early '50s, which eschewed the more traditional chrome bars and slats in favor of a seductive chrome "bullet nose" centered on the front of the car.

Yet what started as a bit of daring and dreaming in the design studio had by the mid- to late 1950s developed into an unrestrained quest to awe and bedazzle an eager car-buying public. American designers hung garish and heavy-handed grille treatments on everything from station wagons to coupes, as aesthetics and practicality took a backseat to glitz and glamour.

While Earl, Exner, and their contemporaries were applying as much chrome and fin as a car could carry, across the pond in Europe, designers like Pininfarina, Scaglietti, and Michelotti were busy designing some of the most remarkable cars of the period. In Europe, grille designs were allowed to evolve slowly, developing

Opposite: The 1956 Packard 400 featured massively chromed grille fenders and headlight trim, offset by a delicate winged hood ornament. By 1956, Packard's days were numbered, but the firm went out in style.

Above: Looking more like a chrome sculpture than an automobile hood ornament, this fanciful swan from the 1954 Packard appears to be bowing to the oncoming traffic.

into a feature that became the calling card for a particular make or model.

Still, this restraint did not stop European designers from making their mark with unique new designs. The 1947 English Austin A 90 Atlantic featured a sweeping streamlined body with a "cyclops," or third-eye, headlight mounted in the center of its grille. In Sweden on June 10, 1947, aircraft manufacturer SAAB produced the first in a line of wing-shaped aerodynamic models designed by Sixten Sason, the model 92. By the time the model 93 was released in 1955, Sason had designed the grille that would identify the SAAB front end through the model 99 of the 1970s and '80s. Although the grille evolved to suit the aerodynamic and other changes in the car's design, the overall shape remained constant—it was the car's signature "face."

Such new and well-conceived trends soon had an influence on American automotive design as well. Ferrari had quickly become the benchmark of European design, and that company's classic "egg-crate" grille became the inspiration for similar treatments back in the States, among them the 1955 Chevrolet. By the late 1960s and into the '70s, virtually all American grille treatments would show some European influence.

 Right: The tasteful and imposing Duesenberg front end. From any angle, this 1930s marvel was a spectacular treat for the eyes. Is it any wonder that the Duesenberg may have inspired a long-used slang term, as in "Wow! That's a doozy!"?

Right: **The 1948 Lincoln Continental Cabriolet, powered by a V12 engine, was the last of the postwar Lincolns to exhibit prewar design. The amount of chrome on this front end foreshadowed what would be industrywide in a few short years. Ironically, Lincoln would take a more conservative tack, when other car makers were running wild with chrome.**

Opposite above: **A true masterpiece of the metalworker's art: the 1933 Ford Cabriolet hood ornament.**

Opposite below: **As Bogey's Rick would say, "Here's looking at you, kid!" The headlight nacelle of a 1930s Ford was a masterfully harmonious union of form and function.**

Pages 18–19: The 1938 Jaguar SS
100 convertible. With its origins
in motorcycle sidecars, the SS
100 was the first Jaguar to bear
the name. Its ability to attain
speeds in excess of 100 mph
(161kph) would forever link
Jaguar with performance: imagine
seeing this classic front end fill
your rearview mirror while you
were motoring through the
Midlands of England, or along
the Mulsanne straight at the
24 Hours of Le Mans.
A fine sight indeed.

Left: The 1967 Camaro. The racing stripes, driving/fog lights, egg-crate grille, and chromed fasteners on bumpers yielded the racing look so popular in the late sixties.

Opposite: In an era of garish fins and way too much chrome, the 1956 Lincoln Mark II offered understated elegance for the rich and secure, who didn't have to advertise their success to everyone they passed.

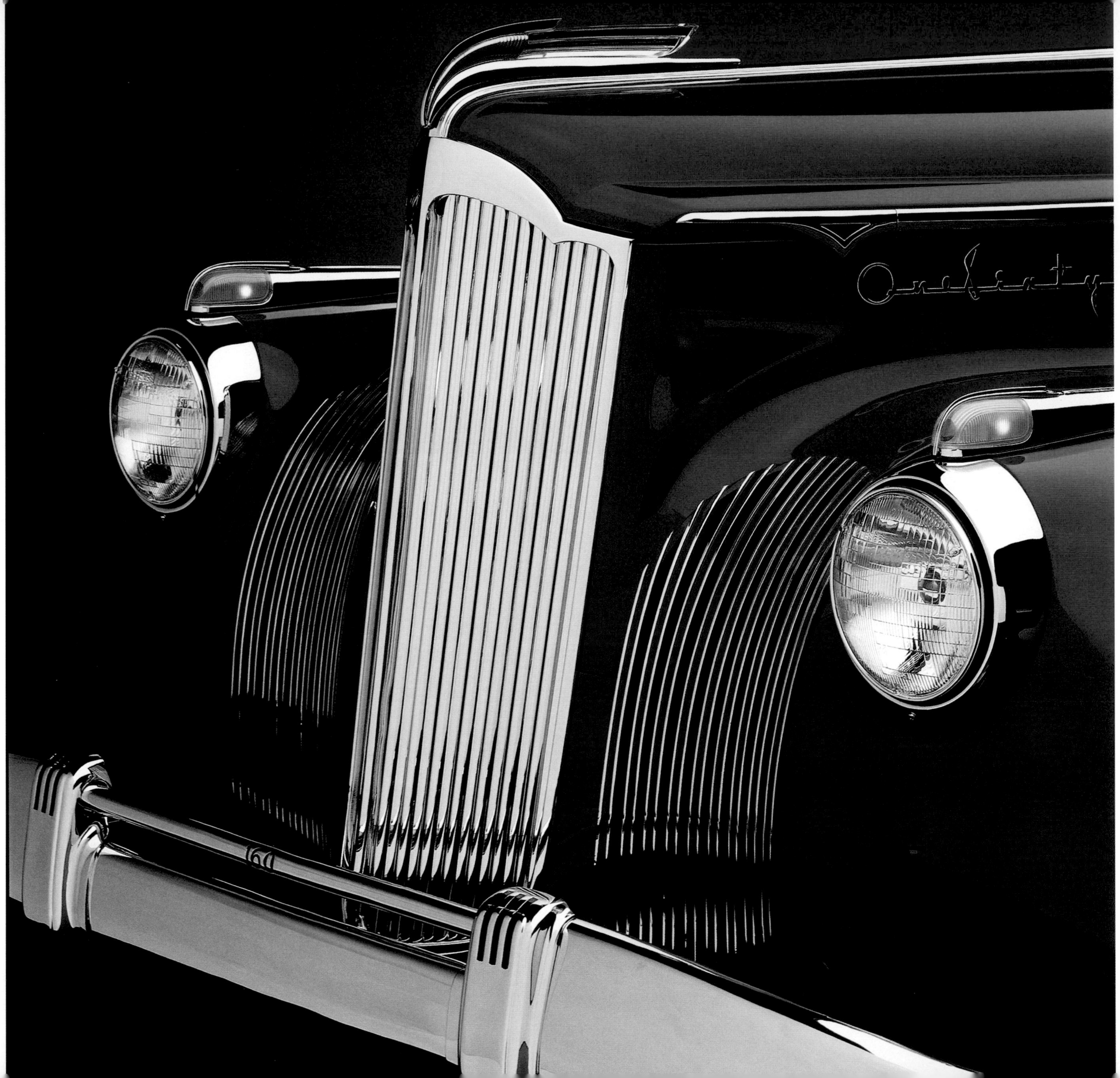

Opposite: The 1941 Packard's front-end treatment was one of the most elegant to come from this manufacturer. It combined a stately, upright appearance with just the right traces of Art Deco styling.

Right: The 1948 Tucker. The engineering of this car literally revolutionized the auto industry. This center-mounted headlight, which swiveled in the direction the car turned, made the Tucker immediately recognizable. Unfortunately, after a run of fifty-one cars, Tucker was forced out of business by its rivals' powerful lobbies.

23

24

Left: The most famous and longest-lived "mascot," Rolls-Royce's "Spirit of Ecstasy" appeared on the earliest models, in the 1910s, and continues to grace all Rolls right up to the present. The mascot and the meticulously hand-crafted radiator grille say at once that this is a Rolls-Royce, the finest car made.

Right: The 1933 Packard typifies the high-end design of one of the best cars built in America.

Opposite: The 1948 Tucker. What might have been, if Tucker had been able to mass-produce this car? Go out to your favorite video store and rent *Tucker*, starring Jeff Bridges—it's the greatest gathering of many of the original remaining Tuckers you'll ever see.

Below: Art Deco styling was not exclusively the realm of the wealthy in the late 1930s. This 1938 Chevrolet, Everyman's bread-and-butter car, features the swept-back line that streamlined just about everything from toasters to radios, buildings, and fountain pens.

Right: Animals have starred as ornaments throughout automotive history. This leaping greyhound on the 1934 Ford was certainly more symbolic of speed than the quail that preceded it on late-1920s and early-1930s Model As. Originally part of the radiator cap, these "mascots" later appeared, as here, affixed to the hood.

Above: A fine study in Art
Deco–inspired design, the hood of
the 1936 Mercedes roadster
featured chrome slats surrounding
the Mercedes three-pointed
star—a successful combination of
streamlined design and instant
brand recognition.

Right: The front end of the 1939
Alfa Romeo Corsa defines sexy,
streamlined Deco design.

Left: **Packard put its best face forward: this design is at once bold and elegant, but also tarted up with the requisite overabundance of 1950s chrome. By the time this 1954 model hit the streets, Packard had fallen on hard times. Its days were numbered but the carmaker continued to build fine-quality, high-end automobiles.**

Right: **This Packard hood ornament is another appealing example of 1930s design.**

Opposite: The Ferrari 250 GTO of 1963. Built as a long-distance racing machine for venues like the 24 Hours of Le Mans, the GTO was Ferrari's last front-engine race car. Extremely rare, the Pininfarina design remains contemporary into the new millennium. It is Ferrari at its best, V12-powered and built for one thing and one thing only—to win races. It is the Italian carmaker's crown jewel.

Right: Even heavily modified by creative, performance-minded hot-rodders, the coupes of the 1930s retained their signature features: separate fenders, slatted hoods, a radiator that looked like a radiator, and freestanding headlights. It is perhaps their front-end design elements that made these coupes so popular with hot-rod aficionados in the first place.

Left: The 1968 Ford Mustang in
Limited Edition Playboy Pink. This
logo would fast become one of
the most famous of all time.

Opposite: The 1958 Edsel had
a face only a mother could love.
The large horse-collar grille gave
this legendarily unfortunate model
a look unlike anything on the
road, and ultimately contributed
to its demise.

Pages 36–37: The 166MM Barchetta
was the first postwar Ferrari. Its
sleek design incorporated an
egg-crate grille that continues to
appear—albeit in more streamlined
versions—on most Ferraris
up to the present.

Left: Behind that Art Deco front end stretches one of the most beautiful Packard Roadster bodies ever designed, the 1930 850.

Right: Even sans chrome, the front-end grille of the 1938 Chevy offered Art Deco–inspired design in an affordable, low-end car. A perfect harmony of paint and chrome—and a most famous emblem.

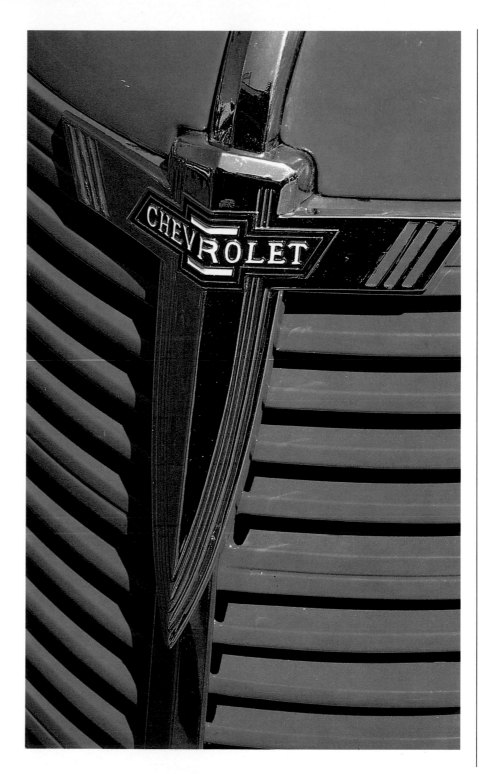

Above: The 1999 BMW M
Roadster. Bulging fender flares, a
larger front chin-spoiler, and an
awesome V8 characterize this
high-performance automobile. The
twin kidney-shaped grilles, long a
signature BMW front-end feature,
identifies the car instantly.

Below: In the 1930s, the V-8 engine came into its own, and power and speed took a quantum leap forward. Even in abstract Deco form, the prow of this Ford hood proclaimed loud and clear just what was lurking underneath.

41

Above: One of two aircraft-inspired hood ornaments on a 1957 Chevrolet. These looked like a fighter jet in a roll and introduced a theme that continued back to the stunning slab-sided fin, the signature of all '57 Chevrolets.

Left: The front end of a 1930s Chrysler demonstrates sturdy and handsome prewar styling.

Opposite: Perhaps one of the most stunning designs ever, the infamous Mercedes 300SL Gullwing. The simple opening in the front, with the three-pointed star seemingly suspended inside, is an elegant take on grille design from Germany's finest builder.

Left: How's this for an Art Deco masterpiece? The 1930 Packard sported this lovely sculpture to point the way for its lucky owner.

Right: Reborn in 1987, Bugatti was still associated with high quality and performance, long the trademarks of the marque. The 1994 EB110 offered race-track behavior with a V12 engine and shot to the top of the Super Car class. The tiny opening in the center of the front intake slats pays homage to the classic prewar Bugatti horse-collar grille. Bugatti's reincarnation was sadly short-lived: in 1994, the marque ceased to exist, this time for good.

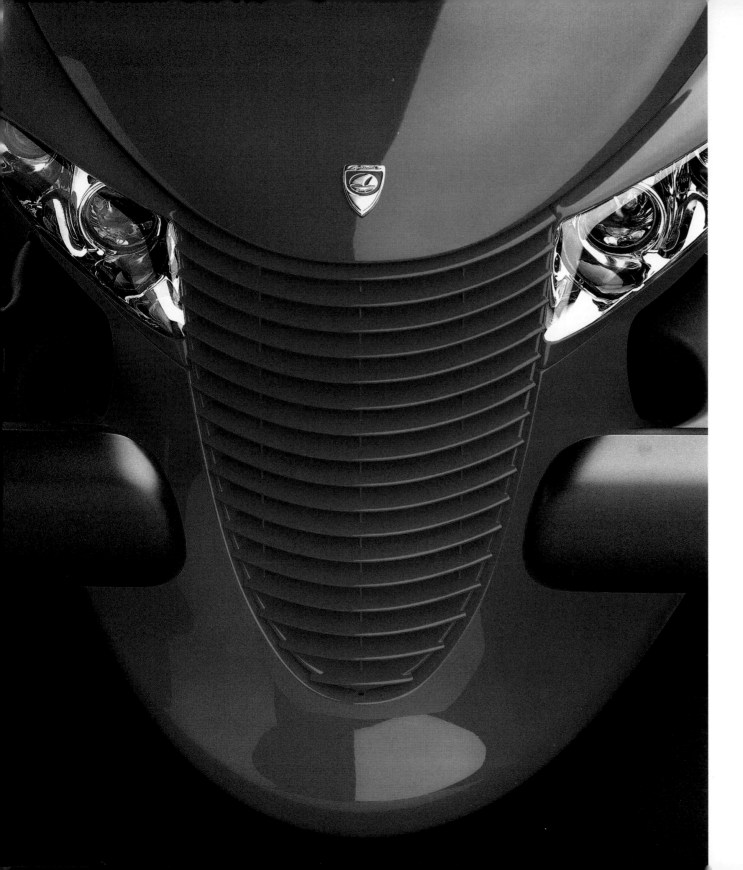

Left: Chrysler continues to push
the envelope on retrostyled cars.
Harking back to the boulevard
hot rod days of the 1950s, the
Prowler is a visual treat. The
grille, though, is right out of
the '30s, smiling almost smugly,
as if it knows it looks like
nothing else on the road.

Right: **The 1959 Dodge Coronet,** typical of some of the decade's less successful design themes, looks like a chromed snarling dog, an ostentatious display of the glitz factor.

Chapter Two

Bringing up the Rear
Fins, Whale Tails, and Other Happy Endings

During the 1930s, back-end designs on American cars were fairly conservative: taillights were usually mounted on top of the fender in a small chrome nacelle, and perhaps there was a bulge in the rear to allow a bit more trunk space. For the most part, though, form followed function out back on most everyday, bread-and-butter car models. Notable exceptions could be seen in the high-priced, low-volume marques like Duesenburg, Cord, and Auburn, as well as European maker Bugatti. These marques featured some of the finest—and, yes, wildest—design themes from the period. The rakish and streamlined lines of the 1935 Auburn "boat-tailed" Speedster, for example, came together at the rear in a prow shape resembling the hull of an overturned speedboat, a popular design theme of the era.

But by the 1950s, society's tastes were turning away from the nautical themes of the prior era and toward the skies and beyond. Sensing the growing love affair society was soon to experience with jet travel and space rockets, GM's Harley Earl defined the American automobile in the '50s, creating his legendary designs and inspiring countless competitors. At the heart of Earl's vision was the fin, a jet age–influenced inspiration that evolved into a craze, spreading

Opposite: **By the early 1960s, fins were on the way out on American cars. That being said, this 1959 Pontiac had not one but two residual fins over each directional signal. Chrome remained popular and plentiful.**

Above: **If you were partial to chrome—as in "lots of it"—in 1957, then the Buick Special of that year would be hard, if not impossible, to pass up.**

eventually beyond America's borders. Although the cars coming out of Europe in the '50s were somewhat conservative compared to the high-flying rear ends of American cars of the time, some designers, the British in particular, were sufficiently influenced by the aesthetic excesses of Detroit's Big Three and answered with designs that featured similarly styled—though slightly more restrained—fins.

Things were quite different at Italy's most respected design studio. During the 1950s, Ferrari defined the sports car, producing shapes that were informed by aerodynamics rather than excess. Featuring flowing and rounded rear ends, with tastefully rounded lights, Ferrari offered a glimpse of the future of the automobile. The 1955 Pininfarina–designed 410 Superamerica Ferrari featured a sleek, finless body shape that would look contemporary a decade or more later.

In comparison to the flamboyance of the previous decade, the 1960s seemed downright conservative in terms of tail design. Nonetheless, the era saw some truly fine tail designs, with the 1963 split-window Corvette Coupe garnering top vote among most enthusiasts. Meanwhile, over in Europe, designers embraced the kamm back. Enthusiasts were horrified when, in 1967, Alfa Romeo chopped off the seductively rounded tail of the Pininfarina–designed 1600 Duetto Spyder. This amputation improved fuel economy and aerodynamics at the expense of a most sensuous and classic design.

During the 1970s, automakers worldwide were left to contend with stringent U.S. government regulations mandating rear-end designs that could withstand an impact of 2.5 mph (4kph) without damage. Already losing sales to smaller and more fuel-efficient imports, American car designers found style low on their priority list when building new models, and, as a result, many of the bumpers on American cars from that period resembled battering rams or chromed railroad ties. But by the end of the decade, designers armed with newly developed plastics and composites would begin to once again revolutionize the bumper, creating streamlined, integrated designs that were at once attractive and practical. By the mid-1980s, incredible rear-end designs were once again rolling off assembly lines, perhaps best exemplified by the 1984 Porsche Turbo, which featured a wide rear end lovingly referred to as a whale tail, which accommodated the widest tires available.

By the time of the economic boom of the late 1990s, a design revolution was in full swing. Retrostyling had become a style of its own, with influences from models past showing up on the newly designed Volkswagen Beetle, Corvette, and Thunderbird, among others. Indeed, what's old is new again, and in the very best of ways.

Above: The 1956 Chevrolet's taillight gave subtle hints of the fabulous fin that would appear on the '57 model. Tasteful, with just enough chrome, it is one of the elements that make the '56 one of today's most sought-after Chevy models of the era.

Opposite: The 1998 New Beetle. This reincarnation of the beloved Bug was a stroke of sheer styling genius, proof of the enduring mystique of the Volkswagen Beetle. Even though the Beetle was absent from the American market for almost twenty years, the new model looks exactly as you'd expect it to, had it continued to evolve over the period.

Opposite: The Studebaker Golden Hawk was powered by a 289 cu. in. supercharged V-8 that put out a respectable 275hp. This was one car from the 1950s on which the fins complemented its aggressive design.

Right: A detail from the 1957 Buick Skylark. The Skylark was a 1953 design exercise: only 1,690 of these stylish convertibles were built. The chrome trim and spears masterfully echoed the wheel arch. Red inlay on the trim and wire wheel was an elegant finishing touch.

Pages 54–55: One of the legendary prewar roadsters from Great Britain, the Jaguar SS 100 boasted fenders separate from the body, a spare mounted on the rear deck, separate headlight castings, and a slotted bonnet. Its shape inspired many postwar sports cars, from the MG-T series to today's Morgans, which still retain the style.

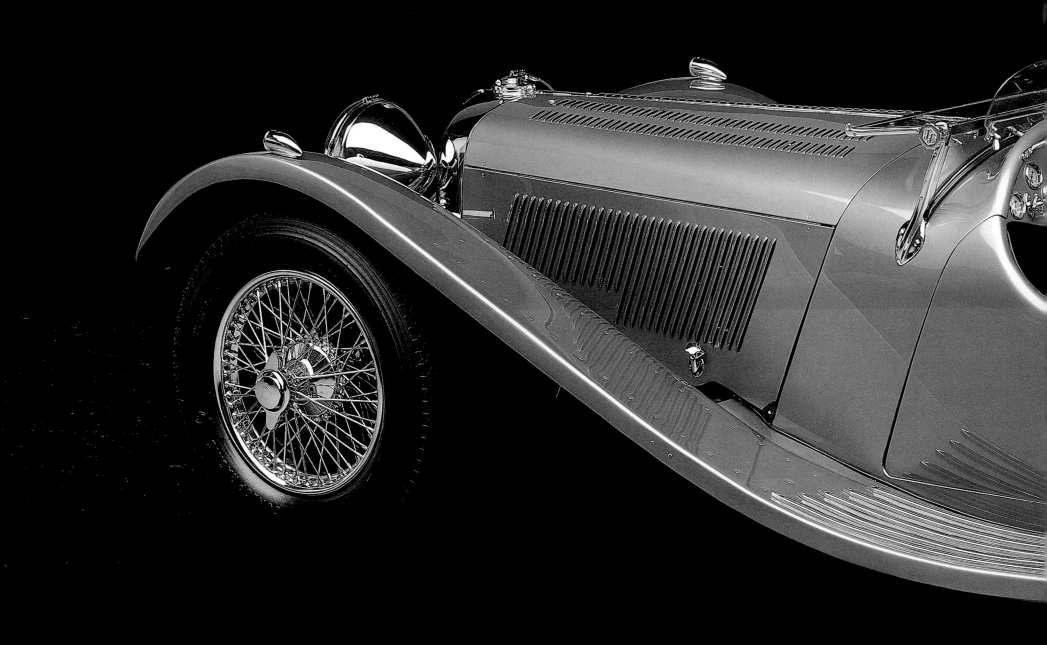

Above: Few tails from the 1950s
were as tasteful or aged as well as
those on the 1957 Chevrolet, its
fluted steel trim recalling the era's
streamlined stainless steel
railroad passenger cars.

Opposite: The tail of the 1957
Pontiac looked sculpted rather
than assembled out of chrome
and plastic. The influence of the
jet age is evident here.

Left: No fin on any other automobile came close to the ones on the 1959 Cadillac. And when fins began to disappear in the early 1960s, it was Cadillac that designed the most assured coda to this inimitable design era.

Opposite: The 1954 De Soto Adventurer Coupe. The Italian design firm Ghia was commissioned to do this styling exercise for De Soto. It featured all the popular American themes of the period—chrome details, overhanging rear end, and enormous chrome rings around the taillights that looked like jet exhausts. One notable feature was the rear window, which slid down into the trunk. The car never went into production.

Below: The Cadillac crest, long America's automotive symbol of status, engineering, and quality.

Right: Coming or going, has there ever been a more recognizable shape than the original Volkswagen Beetle? *Everyone*, it seems, has a Beetle story to share—and the topic often arises. The split-window treatment of this 1950 model harks back to the car's prewar design.

Opposite: **The rear end of the 1959 Eldorado was the very definition of flashy excess: its low-down grille was larger than the grilles on a lot of family sedans from the period. The 1959 expressed status and wealth in chromed spades to a generation of postwar Americans who viewed the Cadillac name as *the* ultimate symbol of success.**

Right: **The 1932 Alfa Romeo 8C Touring Spyder evolved from the previous year's 1750 series; its performance made it one of the best-handling sports cars of the period. From the rear, it exhibits the trademark details of 1930s roadster design: separate fenders, the spare wheel and tire mounted on the deck, skinny tires, and a great view down over the long hood.**

Pages 64–65: **The side view of the 1958 Edsel may just be its best view. At least you can't see the horrendous horse-collar grille and that questionable rear-end treatment.**

Left: Corvette was one of the few models that avoided the fin-and-glitz craze of the 1950s, choosing instead to emphasize aircraft-style exhausts in a most attractive and understated treatment. As a result, late-'50s Corvettes are today coveted as classics and command high prices.

Opposite: The 1950 Hudson Commodore Convertible. The shape of the Hudson, a brainchild of designer Frank Spring, was ahead of its time and like nothing else being produced. Its step-down design was low and sleek, while everything else in 1950 was still pretty much prewar: tall and clunky. The rear end's "bustle look," as the Hudson aficionados call it, refers to a Victorian women's fashion. Despite its brave new design, the Hudson Motor Car Company would pass into oblivion a few short years later.

Left: **There's no mistaking the tail of a Ferrari F40. No mere add-on, the rear wing was a necessary aerodynamic device: under the slatted rear glass lurked a slightly detuned version of the then-current Ferrari Formula One engine.**

Right: **By the late 1960s, the excessive fins of the late-'50s Cadillacs had morphed into a more austere and conservative style, although the slab-sided look paid subtle homage to those wild days of gaudy abandon that defined car design in the 1950s.**

Pages 70–71: **Ettore Bugatti was to prewar sports cars what Ferdinand Porsche is to postwar models: both designers masterfully combined aesthetics and world-class performance.**

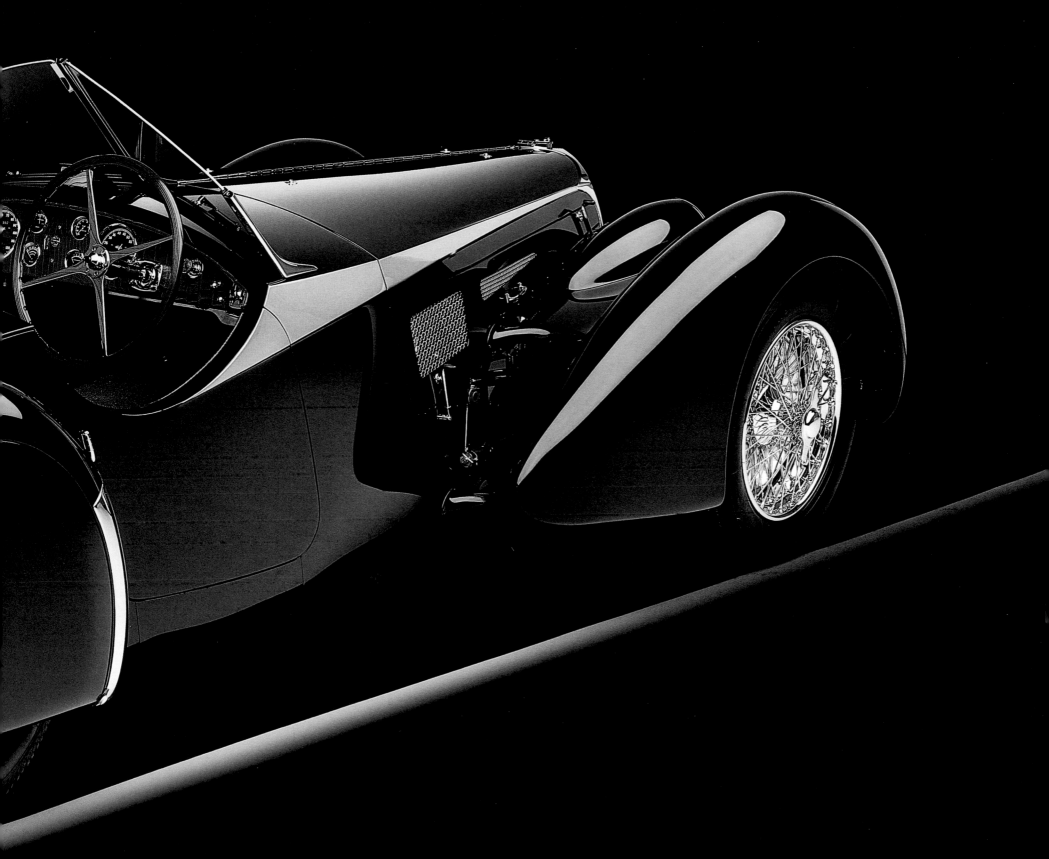

Left: The fins on this Ford
Thunderbird are kissin' cousins of
those on the auto maker's sedans,
convertibles, and wagons, creating
a strong family resemblance across
all Ford model lines unmatched by
any other American manufacturer.

Above: Is this the same company that
created the 1957 and 1959 Chevrolets?
By 1967, the boxy look was in—the
Chevelle Malibu was typical of the
period, with its small taillights aligned
across the rear deck.

Left: The 1959 Dodge Coronet. Is it a chromed bird? Is it a plane? Or perhaps a rocket, thought *Sputnik*-minded Americans. The stepped-back fin appeared on other Mopar models, Chrysler and De Soto.

Opposite: The 1957 Chevy Bel Air. Razor-edge styling and aircraft-inspired exhausts rendered the '57 unmistakable.

Left: Bold, stylized, and chromed, these fins were a dead giveaway that you were following a 1957 Buick Special!

Right: The 1955 Chevy's taillight gave little indication of what was to come in two years. Design changed with incredible speed in the mid-1950s, as planned obsolescence was honed to a science. Offer the public a new body and lots of shiny chrome and they'd scarf up the new models like there was no tomorrow.

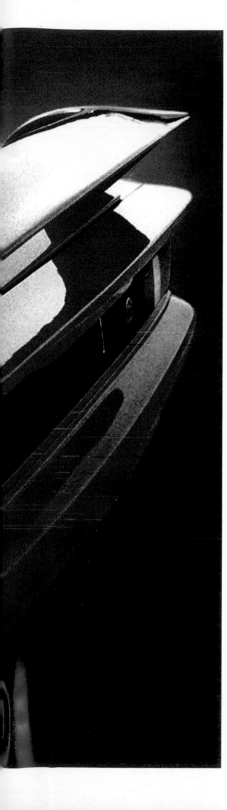

Left: Wings have been popular on sports cars since the late 1960s. This 1999 Lotus Esprit's rear wing looks more like an aftermarket add-on than a well-integrated design element. Still, it does the job, providing the raw performance element that drivers expect in high-end sports cars.

Right: If it was off-center or slightly different in any way, it was usually a Kaiser. This baroque Kaiser Manhattan taillight assembly is fanciful as well as purposeful. Chrome was king in 1954!

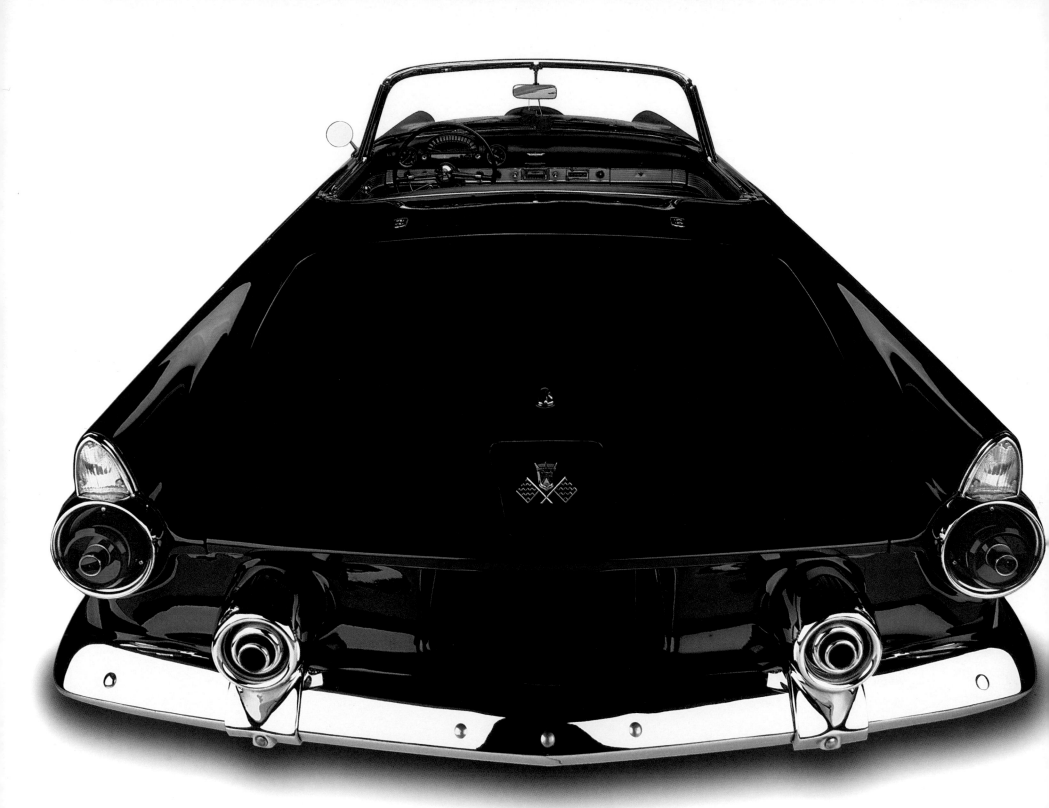

Opposite: From the rear, this
Ford Thunderbird illustrates how
aircraft-inspired elements like fins
and exhaust ports could be
combined with just the right blend
of chrome in an aesthetically
pleasing package. This may be why
the Thunderbird outsold the
Corvette from 1955 to 1957.

Above: Harley Earl, General Motors'
design chief, added aircraft motifs
on many GM automobiles. This
1954 Corvette sported some of
Mr. Earl's more refined references,
such as the small fins atop the
taillight housing, which are right
off a rocket of the period.
Similarly, the exhaust pipes exiting
the body recall those on aircraft.

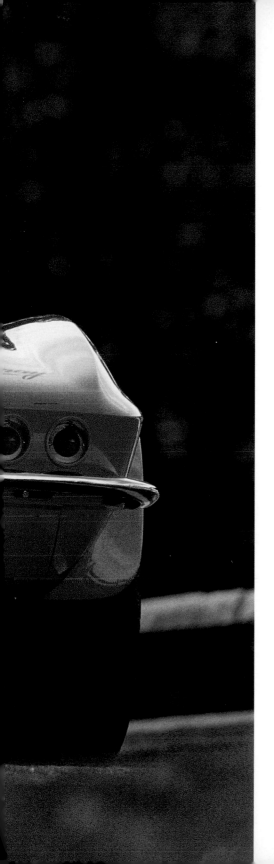

Left: In 1963, Corvette featured the infamous split-window variation on its coupe. The following year, the rear glass was solid, as shown in this '64 model. Either way, Chevrolet certainly got it right: the Vettes from both these years are stunning from any angle.

Right: Understated elegance has always typified the postwar Jaguar sedans and coupes. Beginning in 1975, the XJS was the top of the line; even though it lacked the raw excitement of the XKE series, it was signature Jaguar. It appealed to a moneyed, more conservative clientele who appreciated the performance image of "The Cat" but wanted to arrive in an unrumpled three-piece suit.

Right: The 1996 Porsche Turbo was always the superstar of the 911 models. Blistering performance was first and foremost, developed at venues like the 24 Hours of Le Mans. Compared to those on earlier, 1980s-vintage "whale tail" Turbos, this wing might actually be considered small and conservative.

OCT CALIFORNIA

57 CHFTN

Opposite: The 1957 Pontiac's "wide stance," seen from the rear. Though similar in shape to those of its cousin, the Buick, the Pontiac's fins presented a slightly more restrained appearance.

Right: The new and wickedly exciting Jaguar XK8 harks back to the glory days of the most famous of the postwar Jaguar roadsters, the XKE. Although the XK8's taillight is larger, in accordance with the government-mandated minimum size, it shows its descent from the delicate taillights that graced the rear of the XKEs.

Pages 92–93: Nash, never a big player in the American car market of the 1950s, nevertheless made some rather brashly unorthodox design statements. Devised by noted Italian designer Pininfarina, this 1954 Nash Ambassador Statesman hid its spare tire in an attractive body-colored Continental Kit.

Suggested Reading

Bayley, Stephen. *Harley Earl*. Np: Taplinger Publishing Company, 1991.

Carson, Richard Burns. *The Olympian Cars.* New York: Alfred A. Knopf, 1976

Culshaw, David, and Peter Harrobin. *The Complete Catalogue of British Cars*. New York: William Morrow & Co., 1974.

Clymer, Flyod. *Treasury of Foreign Cars Old and New*. New York: McGraw-Hill, 1957. Damann, George H. *Ninety Years of Ford*. Osceola, Wisconsin: Motorbooks International, 1993.

Damann, George H. *Seventy-five Years of Chevrolet*. Sarasota, Florida: Crestline Publishing, 1986.

Gunnell, John A. (ed.). *Standard Catalog of American Cars, 1946-1975*. Iola, Wisconsin: Krause Publications,1982.

Halberstadt, Hans. *Woodies*. New York: Metrobooks, 2000.

Harding, Anthony, gen. ed. *Classic Cars in Profile, Volumes 1 and 2*. New York: Doubleday & Co., 1967.

Kimes, Beverly Rae (ed.). *Standard Catalog of American Cars, 1805-1942*. Iola, Wisconsin: Krause Publications, 1989.

Norbye, Jan P. and Jim Dunne. *Buick 1946–1978: The Classic Postwar Years*. Oscola, Wisconsin: Motorbooks International, 1997.

Pfau, Hugo. *The Custom Body Era*. Np: Castle Books, 1970.

Ralston, Marc. *Pierce-Arrow*. Np: Tantiug Press: 1980.

Sedgwick, Michael. *Cars of the Thirties and Forties.* New York: Beekman House,1979.

Setright, L.J.K. *The Designers: Great Automobiles and The Men Who Made Them*. Np: Follet Publishing Co., 1976.

Stein, Ralph. *The Greatest Cars*. New York: Simon & Schuster, 1979.

Stein, Ralph. *The Treasury of the Automobile*. New York: Simon & Schuster, 1961.

Wagner, Rob L. *Classic Cars*. New York: Metrobooks, 1996.

Wagner, Rob L. *Style & Speed: The World's Greatest Sports Cars*. New York: Metrobooks: 1998.

Index

Photo Credits

® Don Spiro; pp. 56, 64, 86-87, 92-93
® Richard Cummins; pp 9, 13, 14, 17 top & bottom, 20, 24, 27 center & right, 28 left, 31, 33, 34, 39, 41 center, 41 right, 51, 54, 58, 67, 71, 77, 83, 84
® R. Krubner/H. Armstrong Roberts; p. 44
® Robert Landau/H. Armstrong Roberts; p. 42
® Ronald Cantor; p. 23
® Ron Kimball; pp. 5, 6-7, 8, 10-11, 12, 15-16, 18-19, 21, 22, 24-25, 26, 28-29, 30-31, 32, 35, 36-37, 38-39, 40, 43, 44-45, 46, 47, 50, 52-53, 57, 58-59, 60, 61, 62-63, 65, 68-69, 72, 73, 80-81, 85, 87-88, 88-89, 91
® Zone Five Photo; pp. 55, 75, 78, 90
® Zoomstock; 2, 48, 49, 66-67, 70-71, 74-75, 76-77, 79, 82